First published in Great Britain in 1998 by
Frances Lincoln Limited, 4 Torriano Mews
Torriano Avenue, London NW5 2RZ

First published in the United States in 1998 by
Silver Press
A Division of Simon & Schuster
299 Jefferson Road, Parsippany, NJ 07054

LIBRARY OF CONGRESS CATALOGUING-IN-PUBLICATION DATA
Cave, Kathryn
W is for World: around the world ABC/Kathryn Cave
p. cm.
Summary: Text and photographers depict different parts of the world, from A to Z,
exploring what the land is like and how people live in each place.
1. Geography—Juvenile literature. [1. Geography. 2. Alphabet.]
I. Title.
G133.C36 1999
[E] —dc21 —dc21
[428.1]
97-50515 CIP AC
ISBN 0-382-42113-2 (LSB) 10 9 8 7 6 5 4 3 2 1
ISBN 0-382-42114-0 (PBK) 10 9 8 7 6 5 4 3 2 1

Printed and bound in Hong Kong

W is for World

A ROUND-THE-WORLD ABC

Kathryn Cave

SILVER PRESS
Parsippany, New Jersey

Author's note

If you look at a map of the world, you can find all sorts of things—countries and continents, oceans and rivers, icecaps and deserts. Maps of the world show the planet we live on, the physical world we share.

The alphabet of *W is for World* is full of the kinds of things you won't find on a map. It's about homes, schools, and families, the clothes we wear, the kinds of food we eat. It's an alphabet of people, cultures, customs, and beliefs. In fact, it isn't really an alphabet of one world at all, but of many worlds—too many to count—the worlds of children growing up in places as far apart as Greenland, Jamaica, and Colombia, or India, Brazil, and Mozambique. I hope it suggests both how different the world may look to people of different backgrounds, and in spite of that, how many important things we have in common.

Thank you to Oxfam for their help and expertise in researching this book, and to all the children whose photographs appear (sometimes under made-up names if we couldn't find the real ones).

Aa is for Arturo, Alfredo, Agostino, and all of the children who work.

All over the world, there are children who work. The money they earn helps their families survive. Arturo and his friends are selling samosas—hot spicy snacks —on a street in Maputo, Mozambique.

Bb

is for Books to read,
to treasure, to share
with our friends.

Nur lives on an island in
Bangladesh. There is no
bookshop or library near
her home, so her books
are especially precious.

Cc is for Clothes to keep us cool when we're hot, and warm when we're cold, and to make us stand out in a crowd.

Women in Senegal can buy cloth from all over the world at their local market. They make their outfits themselves, or get a friend or a seamstress to do it. No two outfits look quite the same. The point is to make a splash and stand out in the crowd.

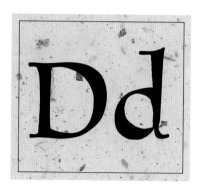

Dd is for Desert, too dry and dusty
for most plants to grow.

Rain is scarce in the desert, and water is very precious. Without it, people, plants, and animals die. The deserts of the world are spreading as the climate changes and people use up the trees and plants that grow around them. Abdou, who lives in the north of Mali, is getting water for his donkeys from a well.

Ee

is for Eyes, which
help us see the world
and each other.

Most of us use our eyes every
moment, from when we wake
until we fall asleep again. Without
them we couldn't recognize colors
or a friendly face. Anyone with
good eyesight, like Oscar, has
something to be thankful for.
Oscar lives in Colombia.

Ff

is for the Food we grow or buy, prepare, and cook in so many different ways.

Whether we eat rice boiled over an open flame in India, oranges fresh from the market stall in Bolivia, or pounded grain in Pakistan, what we eat and how we eat it is important to us. Most important of all is that nobody goes hungry.

Gg

is for Grandfather, gentle
and wise, ready to tell you
a story and give you a hug.

Grandparents are special, no
matter where you live. In some
countries, grandparents live
together with their children and
grandchildren in the same family
home. No one could feel lonely
with a family this big. Sumana
and her grandfather are from a
Tamil community in Sri Lanka.

is for Home,
the place we belong.

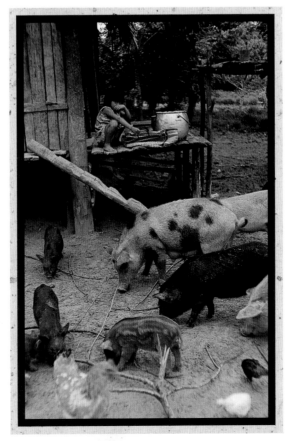

Homes come in all shapes and sizes. For some people, it's a tent, like the one where Hamid and Hameda live in the desert of Sudan. Home may be a wooden shack in a township in South Africa, or a hut in the forests of Brazil. The best thing about a home is having one. Home is where we feel safe and loved.

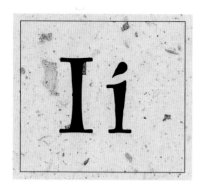

I i

is for Icebergs,
bigger than houses,
floating in the ocean.

Some parts of the world are
covered in ice all year round.
These giant icebergs have broken
away from the icecap that
covers Greenland and are
floating south past the shore.
The water is very cold here, so
although it's a hot summer day,
the boys wear boots to paddle.

J j is for Journeys, long or short, with friends or alone.

No need to journey by plane, or car, or train, or bicycle—many people still travel on foot. These children in Ecuador are setting off to the local school. It's quite a walk, but they have friends to share the journey.

Dominique has no running water at home, so she's carrying it back from the well in a bucket. She lives in a dry part of Haiti, a country in the Caribbean.

Kk is for Kite, to play with on a windy day.

Kite-flying began in China, but now it's popular everywhere. Whole families go out to fly kites together on this windy hillside in Ecuador.

Ll

is for the Lamps
we light at night.

Many homes have no gas or
electricity. After dark, people
use lanterns, candles, or lamps.
This Indian shepherd studies
by lamplight to learn new
ways to look after his flock.

Mm is for Music, to celebrate and to spread good news far and wide.

Mbourel Dia's group of musicians travels from village to village in Senegal, singing songs about the past and about what's been happening locally. They make music on drums, guitars, and whatever else is handy. Who needs a telephone or a radio when you can get news this way?

Nn

is for our Name that tells the world who we are.

Our name is one of the first words we learn. We may be named after a relative or a friend of the family. We may use the same last name as our mother's family or our father's. Some names have a special meaning. This Ethiopian girl is called Muluken, which means 'a full day'.

Oo is for Oceans, where we fish, and sail, and play.

More than two-thirds of our world is covered by salt water. Oceans give us food, like fish and seaweed. Oil and other minerals lie under the ocean. We use oceans to move goods by ship around the world. Where Sharijah and his friends live in Southern India, the Indian Ocean is very rough. The men fish in teams of three.

is for the Peace
we need to work,
sleep, and grow.

Peace gives people the chance to work in the fields and walk in the streets without danger. Children can sleep undisturbed, and wake up to find the world a safe place.

War in Vietnam ended more than 20 years ago. Now people can work in the ricefields without fear of bombs or bullets. The children napping peacefully side by side are in a kindergarten in Nepal.

Qq

is for Queue (pronounced
cue)—a line we stand in
to wait our turn and chat
with our neighbors.

People around the world
queue for all sorts of
things—for food, for water,
for shelter, for a ride. These
women are queuing for
water in a village in India.

Rr

is for River, for splashing, for washing, for drawing water, for taking us from place to place.

Pedro and Paulo live in a part of Brazil where roads are few and far between. The river is the best way to travel, especially for short journeys.

Ss is for Sunrise, time to yawn, and stretch, and get moving.

In India, some people are on their way to work when the sun comes up. Early morning is the coolest time of day in a hot country. These women and children are off to pick jasmine. When the sun is high, the fields will be too hot.

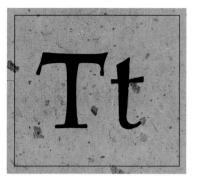

Tt is for Trees that give us shelter and shade from the sun.

Trees are vital to everyone on this planet. They shelter all kinds of birds, plants, animals, and living things too small to see. They take many years to grow, but can be cut down in only minutes. These children in Uganda are having lessons in the shade of an acacia tree while their school is being built.

Uu is for Understanding the world and each other.

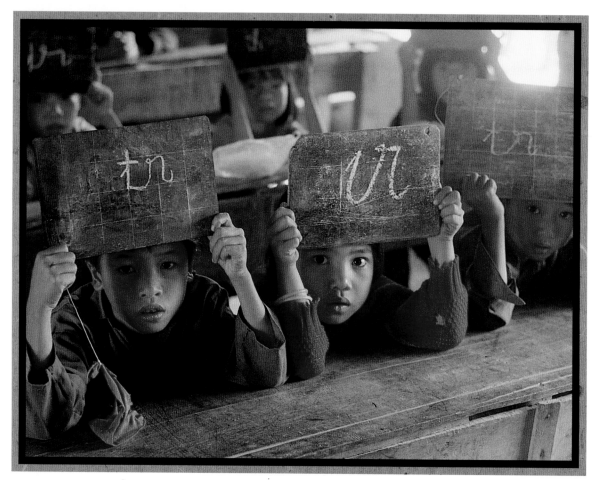

We learn about our world from our parents, our friends, and our teachers, and by noticing what goes on around us. We go on learning all our lives. Hahn and his friends have taken their first step towards understanding the world— they have learned to read. At their school in Vietnam, they write on slates that can be wiped clean and used again and again.

Vv

is for Visitors we welcome
into our homes and lives.

People welcome visitors in
all sorts of ways—by shaking
hands or bowing, by kissing,
or like this, with a hug. These
two friends are meeting to
talk about digging a well in
their village in Senegal.

Ww is for the World we build and share.

Mohammed and Ahmed are making bricks out of clay mixed with manure and straw in Sudan. They will build the bricks into a kiln and use a wood fire to bake them hard. The women are at work in the fields in India. By sharing the work, people all over the world are improving life in lots of ways, making their world a better place to share.

Xx is for oXen to help plow the land and to carry heavy loads.

In many parts of the world, farmers can't afford machines like tractors, so they use animals instead. These Kenyan farmers are using two oxen to plow the land.

Yy

is for Yellow, as
bright as the sun.

In Ethiopia, rain is scarce, so these
women are terracing a field—building
a low wall to keep rainwater from
draining away. The brilliant yellow
of their dresses and head coverings
comes from the vegetable juice they
use to dye the cloth.

Z z is for Zoe. Like every child growing up today, she needs enough to eat, a safe place to live, and the chance to learn, and work, and live her life in peace.

Zoe lives in Jamaica, where many women raise families on their own. Like people all over the world, they help each other, working together to make life better for themselves and their children.

Oxfam believes that all people have basic rights: to earn a living, to have food, shelter, health care, and education. There are ten Oxfam organizations around the world that work with the poor in over 70 countries. Oxfam provides relief in emergencies and gives long term support to people who are working to make life better for themselves and their families.

Oxfam would like to acknowledge, with thanks, the following photographers:
Howard Davies: cover; Nancy Durrell-McKenna: cover background, Z, back cover; Jenny Matthews: A, H (Brazil, hut), T, Y; Shahidul Alam/ *Drik Photo Library*: B; Jeremy Hartley: C, D, P (Nepal,children), V, X; Larry Boyd: E; Rajendra Shaw/*Centre for Development Communication, Hyderabad*: F (India, rice), O, S, W (India, woman's hands); Penny Tweedie: F (Bolivia, oranges); Adrian Neville: G; Paul Grendon: H (South Africa, shack); Sarah Errington: F (Pakistan, grain), H (Sudan, tent), W (Sudan, bricks); Julio Etchart J (Ecuador, children), K; James Hawkins: J (Haiti, landscape), M; Mike Wells: L; Rhodri Jones: N; Sean Sprague: P(Vietnam, field), U; Matthew Titus: Q; Mike Goldwater: R.